THE DEATHS OF ANIMALS AND LESSER GODS

Other books by Gerald Barrax

Another Kind of Rain (Pitt Poetry Series, 1970)

An Audience of One (University of Georgia Press, 1980)

THE DEATHS OF ANIMALS AND LESSER GODS

Gerald Barrax

Volume Four
in the Callaloo Poetry Series
Published at the University of Kentucky
Lexington, 1984

A number of poems in this manuscript originally appeared (or will appear) in the following periodicals, some in slightly different form:

Callaloo: ''The Conception of Goddeath,'' ''From a Person Sitting in Darkness,'' ''Greenhouse,'' ''All My Live Ones,'' ''School Days.''

The Georgia Review: ''Competitors.''

Hambone (Stanford University Committee for Black Performing Arts): ''Poems Like This.'' (formerly titled ''When Things Start Getting Away'').

Obsidian: ''Barriers,'' ''To Waste at Trees,'' ''Portraits,'' ''One of My Own.''

Pembroke Magazine: ''Sleep,'' ''Two Figures on Canvas,'' ''Recital,'' ''Geminis,'' ''Liberation,'' ''The Death of Another Fellow.''

Poetry Now: ''Another Creation,'' ''If She Sang.''

Pot Hooks & Hangers: ''Who Needs No Introduction.''

Works: ''In This Sign,''

Art and front cover design by Guy Davenport

For
My Parents

CONTENTS

ONE

TWO

THREE

ONE

THE CONCEPTION OF GODDEATH

The word *forever* would have pleased him because
He had no name to give the time he had lived,
Each day repeating its unvarying gold.
He knew later that the seasons had not come
Until fear cost him the sun, but had no memory
Of when the days began, no reason to think
Of their end until he saw his animals dying.
Sparrow Hawk dropped from the sky and stiffened
On the ground. Blue Gill and Mud Minnow turned over,
Bloated in the water. Great Reptiles rotted,
Swelled in the sun. Tiger's yawn locked open,
Her serene eyes gone.
                                    He was puzzled, having
Willed none of it. It went on for another
Time of forever until the unthinking moment
Inside the Woman, when with a surprised
New gesture, she touched his face. She touched his face,
Became rigid, violent, muscles pulling him in waves.
He heard their breath come back, saw her eyes close,
And dawn never came more slowly than they
Opened into his ignorance. He had no
Name for what he saw, but his mind exploded,
Awake, memory ticking him away
From ease, from peace, from fable and light. He tried
The clumsy thought *truth*.
                                    He saw in her eyes
All the blazing days of his life; she, too,
Had always been there; if he turned from her
He could see nothing. His hand, with the same grace
As hers, touched her face. Her eyes closed again.
He began seeing through them and remembered
A beast he'd come across, with ribs like hers,
But the flesh melting away into the same

Earth on which she lay, the intense Violet,
Anemone, Foxglove, Flame Flower, Lotus,
The darkest Grass growing in the white cage.
The first time now the sunlight rained, burning
His throat. He could not see her. She shimmered away,
Returned in the raining light. The thing inside
Her burst, exploded backwards into his groin,
Searing inside him up through his burning
Throat. He swallowed that light, raining, the first
Sound that love made.
                Wildebeest, Gazelle,
And Unicorn lifted their heads from grazing.
At the second cry they fled, wheeled back and gazed
At the fear. In his mind, from the ground, the air, the first
Word of the god created answered him.
He closed his eyes to fable, tried truth again.
Phoenix lighted its first fire. No more
Than a stone's throw away in time Odin, Zeus,
Jehovah, Kali, Allah, the Tezcatlipocas,
Shango also awoke with no memory
Before that cry of human, divine need.

COMPETITORS

We still call it mother
and taken without love or care
she bears the weight of our faults,
in her huge orgasms grinding her teeth along her own faults
and shaking our buildings down.
If we counted her bodies and our own
we'd see how little help she needs.
But we do help
with engines invented by cunning men
        catapult, ballista, springal, trebuchet
        throwing swarms of arrows spears stones
        crossbows and Greek fire
to do to flesh what they will.
        At that she sighs in another ecstasy
and turns her winds to widow's work
blowing our buildings down,
knowing we have our own ways to help her
with devilish devices invented by disinterested men
        gunpowder, cannon, mortar, rocket
        aircraft, bomb
to do to flesh what they will.
We help celebrate her five million years dying,
old before her time, logrolling her under our feet,
counting our enemies off the other side,
our enemies counting on time to catch up.
        But it keeps its lead
the thing we call mother.
It turns to the moon
her prodigal lover
back again for her periods of unease
cleansing out her womb with tides that smash down
all we can build or be
without her help.

In spite of all our needs
we do help at her labors.
We deliver bodies to fertilize the body we fight over.
We die to make bodies count for something,
to control the places of slaughter
that the old terror we still call Mother
in the earth wind and water
intended as fields of praise.

BARRIERS

I go out for the news this morning
and find what's left of the slaughtered bird,
guts and wings, on my walk.
I know what did this.
There is someone's black and white cat
that hunts the woods back of our house,
stalking beyond the fence and stealing
some of my admiration for its great cousins
who bring down prey twice their size;
or it perches on a stump
that's a throne among the weeds, a power
in its dominion, but so visible
that I'd wondered if it ever made a kill.
Now here's the proof at my feet
in these black and white wings.
Today I take my stand against relativists
who reduce moral questions to shades of gray.
Things like this belong in the woods,
and that creature had no right to bring its savagery
across the fence and leave it at my door.
I sweep the thing into the grass
before pregnant Helen sees it.
The ants have already started arriving.
It all bothers my stomach at first, but it helps
to see it as a little chicken.
Like the kind we sometimes dress for dinner.

CASSANDRA

She is no wild bird fluttering at a bush
She is a corrupted gypsy swan
She sings with bitter lips to her spiteful god
She shrieks with the pain of his light
She flings away his symbols, the useless glory
Her brain whirls in a storm of prophecies
She terrifies them with her own death
Because men go bewildered in a mist of truth
They will remember her, so lightly killed
They will sicken and die for her songs
They will know it was their desire that destroyed her
They will know it was not a god.

We are waiting for someone like that to come again.

MORE AND LESS

Survivors of war
know best the repeated numb perplexity
that follows grenade explosions within someone else's range;
or the thousand aimless rounds
that people their civilian sleep
with squad after squad of bodies taking someone else's
last step.

But bewilderment follows all through fire,
head-ons, hurricane, structural collapse
with the "Why" after the prayer of thanks
or rage against our choice of deities
for the someone who didn't survive.

Except for ego
or some genetic or learned need
to believe in the design of sparrows falling,
we might answer with the *uncertainty* of human events,
stumbling around the nucleus of death
like electrons in unpredictable orbits
of probable place, speed, energy;
like this leaf falling from autumn today
before another.
Why your race, color, nationality?
Why born? in 1933 and not? when?

When decay or catastrophe collapses all events
into the waiting center,
the single human stake is high enough
to flush minds and hearts free of doubt,
offering the final choice
to pray or curse—if the last ironic flash
shows that chance has played god with the universe.

WHO NEEDS NO INTRODUCTION

Sometimes in the cool of the garden
he walks through the setting that was
his early and, some say, only
success; the birds, flowers, animals
and all the rest whose names he can't
always remember still there,
properties for another try. He picks,
examines a strawberry in amazement, watches
the way the sun comes and goes,
the seasons of the moon. He thinks they
serve him better than the myriad little
theaters that sprang up like weeds
in old gardens and put on
those amateurish spectacles in his name.
The rivalry between them was killing—each
company with its prescribed repertory of roles,
masks, rituals—none of it adding
to his stature. It was all so wearying.

                    Bursting out of the dew
he loafs with snails under the leaves,
admiring the warm sound their moist
muscles make as they go; or listens
in disbelief to a mad mockingbird,
unable to recall the sanity or the whim
in which he had done that. He imagines
that he had stopped there the first
time, and leans against the grass
in the spot light of his last star.

IN THIS SIGN

I

It was already too late for us
When Simon the Cyrenian was seized
And made the first to feel the weight
Of that Man of Sorrows, who shaped the world
To the four corners of his cross.
Then Constantine's sign of conquest finished us.
Born too soon to know the smell of kerosene,
He saw it wrapped in burlap
Blazing in the sky, and on our hills and lawns,
Illuminating the ghastly black things slaughtered on trees.

II

i. Prince Henry's men come down our coast,
Out to prove the roundness of their world.
            We know ours is, have no reason to explore.
            Its circle is the death of ancestors
            Who watch over us from the forests,
            Their births from them and back again.
But Gonzales comes in 1441, finds us and takes Twelve
Away to Portugal. Not enough.
Never enough. They return in three years.
            "And at last our Lord God
            who giveth a reward for every good deed,
            willed that for the toil they had undergone
            in his service, they should that day obtain victory
            over their enemies, as well as a guerdon
            and a payment for all their labor and expense;
            for they took captive of those moors,

   what with men, women and children, 165,
   besides those that perished and were killed.''
Baptisms: 165 washed in the blood of the Lamb
Slaves: 165 washed in the blood of the Lamb.

ii. In 1481 our sphincters tighten for chaos again.
On the Gold Coast, d'Azambuja tells us
They will build a place of worship at Elmina
To bring us their Lord's blessing.
   Do, Lord, oh do Lord,
   Oh do remember me!
We agree. One can never have too many gods,
We thought, when others had come with crescent and sword
And the gift of Allah.
Some accepted. They were allowed to live—
As brothers, we were told; as brothers taken away
Beyond the Great Desert; as brothers
We never see again. Our fathers who art.
Spitting in the face of memory,
We agree to this new god
And they put up their place of worship.

They build a fort, they raise a flag, we hear a mass.

III

i. Enter Columbus, declaiming,
   ''God has reserved for the Spanish monarchs,
   not only all the treasure of the New World
   but a still greater treasure of inestimable value,
   in the infinite number of souls destined to be
    brought
   over into the bosom of the Christian Church.''
Then the Lamb speaks as a Bull from Rome,

And East and West are torn apart
On the horns of an Iberian dilemma.
       Pope Alexander says that Spain shall not enter
       Africa and encroach upon Portugal.
         Spain shall have
       The *Asiento* and the rest of the world.
The rest of the world is yellow and black gold.
Gold everywhere they look.
They sweep through the Caribbean,
First falling on their knees
On the groin of the green earth, to pray,
Then on the Indians,
       Columbus calls them.
But even that god won't put the gold into their hands.
Somebody must work to get it out.
       Columbus calls them Indians. They decline,
They escape to the mountains,
Die of Christian diseases,
Die fighting with arrows against steel,
They are hunted down, like Indians.

Ferdinand speaks in Spanish:
       "In view of our earnest desire for the conversion
       of the Indians to our Holy Catholic Faith,
       and seeing that, if persons subject in the Faith
       were there, such conversion might be impeded,
       we cannot consent to the immigration of Moors,
       heretics, Jews, re-converts, or persons newly
       converted to our Holy Faith unless they are Negro
       or other slaves who have been born in the power
       of Christians who are our subjects and nationals
       and carry our express permission."
In the Islands the "wretch" Bishop Las Casas
Accepts God's gift to the New World,
Proposing that each Spaniard will import Twelve

(that number again) Africans to this Eden,
For the prosperity of God and Country.
His. Theirs.

When there are no more Africans in Spain
They are supplied from Africa.
        They who conquer rule with a rod of iron,
        And our earthen pots are shattered to pieces.

This Eden proliferates in gold, tobacco, sugar.
Trees of Life and Knowledge
Fill the mouths of Europe with the luxury of evil,
Ours with sighs and ashes.

Christian Europe sends ships and fight among themselves
For the honor of saving us who languish in Darkness.
For the *Asiento* and the profit of supplying Spain with slaves.
For the greater honor and glory, for the love of God.

ii. Nations rise against Spain, at last
Jealous of her success in spreading the Word.
French Francis frets,
        "The sun shines for me as for others.
        I should very much like to see the clause
        in Adam's will that excludes me from my share
        of the world. God did not create these lands
        for Spaniards only."
Sir William Cecil blasphemes, says the Pope
Has no right to divide the world
And not give any of it to England.
Elizabeth declares that the sea and the air are for all men.
Hakluyt says that with the assistance of God
(with a little help from Hawkins and Drake)
The Queen will increase her dominions,

Fill her banks, and he uses the Word
Reduce
Many pagans to the faith of Jesus.

Britannia grows fatter and whiter
On her diet of Black flesh,
Cements the stones of Liverpool with blood.

IV

i. It's the time of the Second Coming,
We feel his weight again.
Jesus sails the Middle Passage.
Sailing to Birmingham
Where Baptists bomb churches and children's bodies.
Sailing to Boston
Where Catholics bomb bussing and children's minds.
Sailing to Jonestown
Where a self-proclaimed Living God commands
His own slaves, "Bring the babies first"
To the sweetened poison of his power.

Jesus sweetly sounds his name in the believing ear
Of Captain John Newton
(later reverend and psalmist)
who clutches his Bible to his expensively-suited breast,
Preaches two services each Sunday from the deck
To the legitimate majority in the noisome hold
Via TV sets provided by the Company.

Jesus walks the waters, leaves tracks of fire
To guide the shark-disciples—those perfect, silent
Witnesses that follow the ships, waiting
For the desperate men who prefer death

In their own dignity; in their own hours of
Decision they make their leaps of faith
Back into the pure, innocent savagery of
Nature's razor-tooth mouths.

ii. Jamestown,
We come to Jamestown.
In time our sweat and blood bloat
The lean vampire mistress there
Into the Great Whore of Memphis, Charleston,
Mobile, New Orleans, who wallows
In her beds of cotton, stuffing it between her legs
To make her ravaged abomination sweet
For the merchants of the earth.

> *Who are these coming to the sacrifice?*
> *To what green altar...*

Slaves of love and fear,
Slaves of genuine devotion to another white god
Who betrays them again, in green Guyana,
Commands them to "die with dignity"
In a White Night orgy of murder and suicide.
How green
Africa was. How Black
Her maidenhead. How red the altars.
Jesus, how the ships come,
To JamesJonestown, JimCrowtown,
Jesustown, to "America for Jesus,"
Congregations for the Lord in the holds,
Vats of cyanide for the Last Supper.

In Virginia the Assembly legislates,
The churches cheer assent that

> "Baptisme doth not alter the condition of a
> person

as to his bondage or freedom..."
Baptisme doth not alter.
     "   "   "   "

A bishop in Africa languidly waves his hand,
Baptizes slaves going down to the sea in chains,
Knowing it does not alter.
                    Nat Turner! Nat Turner!
                    Do you hear? Do you hear?

                              V

i. The issue of the Harlot's womb
Fight among themselves.
Some believe it's to free Christian slaves,
But it's as much a merchant's war to depose the King
Who keeps the Whore's bed pure and white with Cotton.
Then they who were conquered among themselves
And ground into the earth in humiliation,
Wash their robes in blood, wear them
To hide their nakedness in the night,
Reclaiming their wasted land
In the flaming sign of Constantine.

ii. The War ends. The wars go on, the Knights of the Cross
Ride Terror and Murder, a two-horse race,
Into the next century, out of the night,
Out of their sheets, into magazines,
TV interviews, public shootouts,
Perfunctory guest appearances in American courtrooms.
Their Miss Mary
(blonde, sweet, petite as jockeys must be)
Promises to fix the niggers' bacon
By riding all the horses of the Apocalypse at once.
The symbol is the same. It means the same.

Now the odor is familiar to Constantine.
He knows the stench.

iii. Now this is the only true miracle ever witnessed:
Black people also worship and love this God.
Who has let them drown in their blood,
And His.

ONE OF MY OWN

I have a god
Not like yours
Right for me
Small for my pocket
A Yingyang god/dess
Olorun and Onile
Halved down the middle
Good to me when I'm good to you
And through my pocket pleasures me
With divinest fingers—
Immediate reward when memory fails
To curse you for the poisoned bread your children eat—
The hand of the other half is a razor,
And when I'm not good
My little god/dess gets me living in this life
And slices another nanometer
Through my dickstring.
What more would you
Need to know
To love?

SLOW DRIVERS

Smug
or timid
not always the old
behind the wheel
they sit right
in the middle of the Law
as if it belongs to them;
as if they will inherit
what's yours as well
with your life;
keep you behind them
on narrow roads
hours, days
it seems
all your life!
as if it belongs to them;
it's not that you're reckless
or foolish
or would have them
that way, equally dangerous;
but you must be getting on, getting on
not loitering behind them
where they bait
your fury
and impatience across double lines
into blind
curves
making you wait
wait
wait
wait
wait until you savor the heady salt

of risk on the palate
and pull out
seeing death
in their eyes
when they smirk
at you
as you
pass

SPIRITUALS, GOSPELS

Nothing on earth can make me believe them.
I cringe before the weary forgiving
of that lord whose blood whose blood drowned our gods,
who survived the slave pens
where, thrown in by the masters
as bait to control the chattle,
they nevertheless took him, made him blacker
almost than the masters could endure.
Yet still today, still they sing
to be washed white in his glory, sing
of a bitter earth where my confusions deceive me
    with sweet seasons at my door,
    with dream or memory of savanna and plain
       where the lord is elephant and lion;
       jungle where the deaths of lesser gods
         feed back into its own resurrection;
       canopied rainforest, all that life in the trees
as this earth's heaven.
And whales sing in our oceans.

Yet my own blood weakens, freezes
at their sound, the "unearthly harmonies"
alone probing the faith in my doubt,
making me fear the joy that for the duration of the music
crushes resistence utterly, utterly.
And I know that's who I am, what I am
when the souls of Black folk sing.
While the Soul of Black folk sings.

FROM A PERSON SITTING IN DARKNESS

Very deadly serious, the religious white Christian
lady on TV said God wanted this country
to bomb the Devil out of whatever Yellow Evil
disguises itself as old folk and children.

But the rain,
the rain in trees is a harmony of single drops
on single leaves.

It does not hear me,
the heathen, rage, or the godly rant
their rituals, taboos, formulas, chants
for the gods of every conception.

Cancer cells hear nothing
in spite of prayers,
dividing between love and fear with
        admirable efficiency
into the gods that people heavens and hells,
killing grounds,
nirvanas for the just and wicked.

Divines and scholars debate
Creations
and Last Things, angels die,
dance on subatomic stages.

The swaddling giant GIGO
spews out with terrible efficiency

[GIGO: ''garbage in, garbage out,'' Garbled input to a computer
  produces a garbled output.]

another generation of divines, missionaries at
    the door,
TV evangels with fatuous smiles such as
who say, ''The difference between this
    country
and the Comma Nests
is we have God.''

Thus the male of the species delivers himself
when ''this country'' was bombing the Devil
out of his lady's Yellow Peril, for God.
You might think that's what *he* was talking
    about,
but No, not them, or the Red American Indians
or the Black American Slaves
or the Brown American Anybody
who would've been glad to know that one day
there would be such a difference:
we have God.
But No, this Christian American serious white
very deadly wanted to pray in school.
No. Wanted their children to pray.
No. Wanted my children
to pray to their deadly god in their language,
not knowing how dangerous it is
to erect towers to that peevish One
who shattered common speech into GIGO's
    babel,
scattered man over the face of the earth.

No (the trees). He is everywhere
betrayed by the commonness of his guises,
staked on the dunes between Arab and Jew,
whimpering and hiding in terror from

Protestant
and Catholic bombs on the Emerald Isle.

No, the trees do not heed them,
nor spiders, worms, or cockroaches
locked in their eternal mortal dances
who will inherit what is left of the earth.

What is left of the earth,
counterpoint to the harmony of rain and trees,
the death of GIGO,
the Third Coming will be
in the heart of the atom
(you have been looking in the wrong direction).
All the qualities of the Sacred
are in the Power of the strong force,
so clean, so pure, it holds together
the mutual repulsion of its components
and what church has ever done that?

The Danger of the Sacred
is Goddeath, at the heart of the nucleus
(ask the Japanese, ask the Japanese).

The Mystery of the Sacred
the elusive quarks, Goddeath's angels,
the houri of Allah, minor deities of the Pantheon,
attributes of all gods,
Up, Down, Strangeness, Beauty, Charm,
and the Truths of all gods.

The Secret of the Holy
is hidden in the confinement of the quarks,
their enslavement to Goddeath
who will free them at man's peril
as the Japanese will testify.

The Square Deific of nature's forces
is nonsecterian, at least as reasonable
as other systems, the beauty of the unified field
at least as lovely as any other,
but never mean, hypocritical, murderous
(ask the West African what happened to his ancestors.
Ask the Native American what happened to his land.
Ask the Person Sitting in Darkness what happened to his
    light).

Why not? Why not? I'd like to ask them
to clarify one thing: Is that the only difference,
to have God? I think they were being modest.
But the alternative is GIGO.

ONE MORE WORD

The universe already thrashes
in a big fishnet of words
because everybody thinks nothing is
and nothing had without a name

so I named her a word
that hummed in the wetness of a bad night
because she was escapable
and undiscoverable

as the universe in a fishnet
and my hands were wet for her
but the naming was as good
as when God said

"Give them names Adam"
and Adam named
better than anyone ever
until I named her Lover

in a bad night blowing wetness
and the universe kicked at the net
in a storm
and the thunder said Never.

ANOTHER CREATION

In Egyptian myth Atum-Re
masturbates into the primordial mud,
life begins, and there is another creation.
And why not? But just as my hunger and doubt

had almost become reconciled
I learn the joke that's the meaning of it all.
Now I see the gods, each solitary,
straddling the universe,

busy hands stroking myriads of suns and letting go,
speechless with the gift of laughter
that makes us like them,
because without the redundancy of creation

immortality is a lonely business.
Like them I'm tempted to laugh
if I find that what I have left
in my hands is a poem.

TO WASTE AT TREES

Black men building a Nation,
My Brother said, have no leisure like them
No right to waste at trees
Inventing names for wrens and weeds.
But it's when you don't care about the world
That you begin owning and destroying it
Like them.

And how can you build
Especially a Nation
Without a soul?
He forgot that we've built one already—
In the cane, in the rice and cotton fields
And unlike them, came out humanly whole
Because our fathers, being African,
Saw the sun and moon as God's right and left eye,
Named Him Rain Maker and welcomed the blessings of
    his spit,
Found in the rocks his stoney footprints,
Heard him traveling the sky on the wind
And speaking in the thunder
That would trumpet in the soul of the slave.

Forget this and let them make us deceive ourselves
That seasons have no meanings for us
And like them
We are slaves again.

SYMBIOSIS

You have been tricked out of your element
by versemakers and songwriters; keep them
as hostages for their ignorance and let's exchange
means of survival.

I'll give you what I've used up,
or has used me, and you'll undress
the way trees do in that world better
without us.

Here, Poem, is hate. Here is evil,
and fear. I give them as freely,
as imperatively as you do the itch of summer's hot weeds
and the white fat things

you hide in leaves. Your cacophony
of birds is fair exchange
for the sorrow we feel at the loss of days,
however they go.

Your swarms of gnats dissolve in our tears,
we wink with your butterfly wings at our own cruelties,
our bellies growl when you rumble overhead,
and the thunder

with which you fill vacuums
is indistinguishable from our farts.
We try to deceive you with success
and you expose us,

scurrying on possum hands into our hollow hearts
and fastening your teeth there.
Ah, Poem, we should be true to each other
because an acorn will do

for what genuine faith there is.
Let's celebrate this truce then

for we have become what we are
in creating each other,

I more than ever when I didn't know
where we were going, or why.

POEMS LIKE THIS.

When things start getting away
Those first bites of time
Come out of sensations
That once set the hooks in the brain—
The lines slackening,
Inevitably losing the taste of the bait:
See how deep down and far out
The mind has to go from the bank
To bring back real bubbles for the tongue,
The most stunning pain,
The authentic feel of penetration.
Forgive me:
Even under the lull of those yellow sheets,
Yellow light,
I knew the sharks would come
To feed in the pool that flooded your room.
And even then I was thinking of the right words
For the small tactile things
That would nibble at my mind's version
Of the way things merely felt
From one feeling to the next.
Forgive me:
While you were away from me I was inside you
Trying to remember how deep,
How warm and slick, how cool.
It hasn't kept the sharks away.

SLEEP

I follow her in the broken rhythms of fallow nights
scattering ruined dreams behind her
violent her eyes, the moon
black black sea, the sand
at all ungodly hours she takes as sacrifice
enough words and lines to appease any reason
able lover
and words escape me
like butterflies from the hollow of hands
to adorn her. She wears them
with negligent care.

> (Beside me Helen turns swallowing back
> saliva collected in the pocket of her cheek
> moves under the currents of her sleep like a seal
> following the scent of my consciousness
> moves under her senses
> feeling for the rhythm that I imitate,
> breathing sleep.
> and satisfied she goes under again
> surrendering to her rival's presence
> the warm smell of her own sleep)

Stalking I follow her naked feet
along the edges of composed dreams.
By dawn
too languid to dance the incantation,
she summons the waves with heavy gestures
and opening her thin array turns and waits for me
at last: *Dear heart*
 how like you this?
and laughing scatters
my words like torn off butterfly wings
on the belly of the sea.

TWO FIGURES ON CANVAS

Here in this foreground of sunny Italian fields
She accepts exile as obligation to art.
This one, as all the others,
Has brought her here for his own need
From her harsher land beyond those background towers
Where even a stable and clean straw served
The kind of need they all understand.
He smiles in appreciation at his image of her.
And she, in spirit, must smile because she is aware
Of her renascence among women,
And is woman enough to smile.

She takes and comforts the child.
She assumes her pose from habit, endurance.
She accepts the gambit of heavy satin gown
In fashion with a wistful fancy
For the extravagent cascade of solemn Latin and feudal
      music:
But she laughs at his need for those moons,
For those pancake haloes.

PORTRAITS

On the four-to-twelve shift
on the open door of a locker
a pinktipped kneeling nude
cups, lifts, and squeezes her
self in hands too small
for her own abundance of glossy goodness.
Her smile is warm, sincere.
She is perfectly innocent.
Scotchtaped below her
is a longhaired man with the saddest
blue eyes, too much a gentleman to look up,
but innocently ahead, his hands
pointing the eye to the exposed
incredibly red dripping heart.
He is perfectly serious.
Who wouldn't be proud of a daughter like that?
What a blessing to have such a son.

RECITAL

Halfway back into our cups that night,
the party breaking up,
I heard him say to someone, "I love the sound
your ears make when they wiggle."
I would've known him better for that,
but in all these years we've moved
in different circles of unknowing,
seldom touching: his music, mine words.

When I heard him play last night I knew
the flute must be the right instrument for a man
with the ears to hear things like that.
With his covered by his hair
I knew who I thought him to be,
but more human than that halfgod—
though less than we because he both heard and played
the music he made in us, and moved us in our private
      spheres
to make us more like him,
and the gods whose ruins we are—
whose music is the purest thing left in us.
It still haunts us sometimes from the woods
and still defies imitation: but because he hears
it and tries for us, he helps make us
the best we'll ever be.

                                        (For Don Adcock)

LOVERS

They have been our mortal fools
Since we stood erect, cooked meat, made gods—
Perhaps winning our first laughter
With their windy breathing, their verses,
Their keepsakes, their plagues of anniversaries.
Even now, wave after wave of the air we breathe
Is broadcast with the babble of their ballads,
Making us unwitting celebrants
Of their discovery that robins sing,
The moon shines, violets grow, spring
Arrives, summer endures, and trees and seas
And breezes whisper, all for them. And all

Stop, fade, die, are mute, mocking, when love is gone,
Absent, late. Theirs is no ignoble or trivial pain
That, little less than death,
Has such wide capacity and power
To turn bitter, curse man, beast and stone;
Makes desolation of vast seconds that pinch the brain
To despair, suicide, murder. Yet sometimes in rare
Madness, or pure sanity more awesome,
One will force its shape and sound into an art
That chokes laughter when we recognize
The single human image of its transfigured wisdom.

THREE

GREENHOUSE

First a fable, and then the truth. We sensed
The execution of the plants at their stands
As they guarded us at the door and frozen window
From the light's surprise entrance to the darkest room
We'd known—as if an evening star had collapsed
Into the house's basement room where we
lay dazed in the singularity of a black
Hole in time; our bodies' gravity twisting
Space into the bed's depression, we cancelled
Natural laws, displaced all other matter
And light into the opposite system, beyond
Our control and caring. But when that light
Exploded past our plants faster than its
Own limit, we turned from each other's arms to the sounds
We imagined: ghosts of footsteps overhead,
And Venus's plant, the sundew, pitcher plant,
Cobra lily, sidesaddle flower and butter-
Wort shrieking warning silences and dying for us.

First the fable, and now a truth. But one
Is as strange, has as much charm, color, and beauty
As the other. What matters is the energy of
Its telling, else why *do* the heathen rage,
The godly rant? In truth, they are the same
If based on what we see (even through our
Instruments) and most of all, feel, or expect
One day to prove on the senses. It does matter
That matter is, and that what matter isn't
(Except energy and the unified field) is not.
This is truth: an elegy for whatever died
From neglect while we made love. That night "the music
Of the spheres" was organ music, and when the pipes
Burst, the poor devils froze to death in their places.

We were in the darkest room we'd ever
Known, a true house, a real room, and even
Though half buried in a hillside, was neither
A Swelling in the Ground, nor monarch Thought's
Dominion—not those symbols. It was our darkest
Room because when I put the light out (an
Ordinary light) we had only each
Other, nothing but the comfort and solace
Of our bodies, bodies no denser than all
Ordinary matter and would rot in graves
Less intensely dark than that room where we
Could have stared openeyed forever, forever
Blind waiting for something to emerge,
Reveal itself, take shape. It was that absolute.
The desperate hunger of our bodies, the need
For simple touch, for light, for dark in which
To find the truth about our need—that's what
Devoured the light and left the moon hollow.
That's why the dark was so real: we discovered
That deprivation in love is hunger, is pain
Too common, too necessary to sublimate in fables.
That was truth's light and dark: the necessity
Of pain in our world to make the joy of its
Complete reversal in each other's love with
Even the most primitive harmony that sets
Us apart from the ghostly lives upstairs:
The smooth surprise of tongues in our mouths; our hands
And backs shaping themselves to their own curves and
Hollows from their instant recall of absence.
And it was we and not the spider, coffee,
Coleus, philodendron, African violet,
English and devil's ivy who sang God God
I love you in that dark, because in none
Of the perfect days of unvarying gold had we
Seen so much. That was the truth. Now the fable again.

ALL MY LIVE ONES

Penny accepted the Alabama neighbor's green meat,
Died in our swept-dirt back yard
Near the black wash pot, her brown spot penny-
Side up. My mother's dog, but like
All pets, with no sense of justice:
After forty years she still haunts
Me, innocent of her death, with
These images. My mother en-
Trusted to me the folly of love,
The daily care of caring for them,
And the rest were all mine to lose,
Mockery in their dying
And more than fear in running away.
Rex, ears clipped, tail bobbed, escaped
Into Pennsylvania nowhere
In a cloud of flea powder for no reason
That a twelve-year-old could know.
Micky Midnight, the stray gift to me,
Sick in bed from school, black
As only cats can be, stuck it out
Only long enough for the perfect name
And took it with him.
Fulton (after Sheen the bishop
For his round skull cap), my one canary
Died so soon after he'd learned to sing,
Finally, that I wondered if song
Were worth the cost. And last: Sinbad.
One morning before Pharmaceutical Latin
In nineteen fifty-two I watched him die
My nearest death between my absent brother's
Bed and mine, stretched out, rasping, so closely
Watched I knew and remember which half-second
Distemper tore the last breath out.

But the people: how different.
Since nineteen thirty-three
I've been the key to immortality:
All it takes is loving me:
Both parents, who had me
When they were young; the brother
Who left me there that morning
Alone when that dog died;
A wife who let me go
With her life, our three sons;
Another wife bringing
Her hostages to fortune,
Two daughters; all the lovers.
What will I do?
They are all here. At my age what will I do
With only a bird and a dog long ago?
I cried for days. For days and days.

"SCHOOL DAYS"

Her surprise gift is a photograph,
A six-year-old with an absurdly large white bow
Atop severely combed-back hair.
"When I saw it, I thought it was my sister."
I look at them
Astonished by the woman I know
Waiting in the child's eyes and mouth,
In whose repose I fight the lure of blood
Into forbidden vessels.
Yet she had not recognized herself
Coming back from the past
Had become her own sister.
But because she is here now
I am continually re-making myself,
The past no more immutable than one's identity.
       I hear the taped despair of old music
       below the current of familiar frequencies.
       Like arctic terns guided by infrasonic surf
       thousands of miles away, my memories
       make the long migrations between the poles
       of future and past. I take her back there
       to the boy, give him a glimmer of her
       waiting with all that love, filling in
       some of the empty spaces. Only music
       gives me the bridge to the chasm of self-pity
       I felt hearing Johnny Ace's "Saving My Love for
          You,"
and "Never Let Me Go"; throttled to romantic
delirium by the syrupy strings of Aquaviva's
"Beyond the Next Hill"; never able to keep my hands
from myself, but never in joy. In the collapse
of present and future into my old discontent
we change that,

becoming our own and each other's parents,
children.
From the picture to the woman, to the paradox.
If I had known, I may not have needed her.

GEMINIS

Gemini (the twins): the third sign of the zodiac. In
Egyptian and Greek mythology it was symbolized by two
goats and two children, respectively.

I

They've tried to reckon too
　　　little with the rest of us.
If they neglect their duty,
　　　the children will be the mirrors
in which their room
　　　may prism all our disasters from one

II

Wives, husbands; guiltless lovers, goats; we're one
More than the "usual three"—the two
 Fraternal and identical pairs born in the mirrors
Of our own bodies and minds, duty
And love zodiacal ghosts pursuing us
To meet and twin our souls in each month's room.

Within the moons' circles, we meet in a room
Where each brings a risk that's one
Half the embryo implanted in us;
Where you and I grow and learn to
Defer payment of habitual duty
To the household gods, the ghosts who haunt our mirrors.

We turn them to the wall, but the ceiling mirrors
The sun, our solstice arriving in the room

To inaugurate the reign of another duty—
To love's little deaths our risks have won.
Lust or innocence, twin goats or two
Children, what mythology can ever do us

Justice? Look up or down, Love, and see us,
Souls set free, wedded in mirrors
We turn to face each other, two
Men, women, times two born in the room
Where our bed's first blood christens us one,
Where the sun's red eye is blind to all other duty.

We take the human risks of love and duty
Desperately contesting the four of us,
You and I, he and she in one
Ambiguous circle, a trick of mirrors
Blinding them to us, giving us room
For this heresy of love dividing by more than two.

Husband, wife, friend, and lover, we have too
Many needs to be baffled by duty
Alone; the miracles waking in this room,
In these speechless bodies, confound us
More than our own abstractions, in mirrors
That show love out growing restriction to one.

III

Jazz plays in our room. It pulls us one
Beat beyond their hearing: the music
Of our matrix, out of which the circle
Of identities, out of which love doubles its hands
And we can not tell whose love
Has touched us, in whose minds we have become the
dreams.

"Long before you came, I had been having dreams.
At night I would lie beside him, and someone
(You? All right.) would come and make furious love
To me. I would wake empty as the wind's music
And pull him onto, into me. The hands
I felt were already shaping that triangle into this circle."

"That *was* me, freeing us from her circle
Of guilty fidelity, of dreams
Of me as I never was; those hands
Were mine, feeling for you, for someone
Who returns a body's touch; that music
Was your twin's lament for a lover whose love

Reaches her hands." Still, they are present in our love:
An archer, her aim at duty's circle
Is deadly; blind to forgiveness, deaf to my music.
And he swims like a fish both ways across our dreams;
Never imagines not returning to that one
Familiar cove sheltered with the care of your hands.

Is it your touch or my own, his or hers that hands
Us these brief deaths? In these mirrors, Love,
We don't know between whose limbs which mouths have
        won
This pleasure: my clone, your twin, this androgynous circle
Brings us out of, into our selves as sleep dreams
Its self; as the mirror's echo of itself is the echo's music.

We play jazz in our rooms. It's the mode, the music
Of our invisibility, the wine our hands'
Mystery transubstantiates into our blood's dreams
Of finding the other half, twin whom our soul loves,
Who won't let go. Jealousy is the cruel circle
For those who love us: what they can't lose can never be
        won.

IV

What they call "music"
  may be dirge for their selfish dreams.
But it won't be us, their goats, who will have won:
  we have the kids, whose hands
can make the only circle
  strong enough to keep all our love.

IF SHE SANG

I would feel better if it were song I heard:
in the kitchen, amid the harvest of utensil noise
she sows around her like dragon's teeth;
or in the corner of our room
where she stitches to herself, quietly
until she bursts into speech,
so far from both of us
that a third person is its only possible medium.

"What did you say?"
I sometimes challenge and retreat,
taking the risk of intrusion
because no alarm that brings someone who loves us
is false.

Yet I would feel better
if she sang.
I understand song and could enter
uninvited into its world;
but in her moments of self
and counterself is a dimension with room
for the two only, where even love
is suffered with the patience reserved for fools.

DARA

When they start pulling you out
The anesthesiologist tells me I may look.
I stand and look over the tent
That hides your mother's body from herself.
I look and see
The slick wet head, deceptively black,
That will dry to your nappy red.
Tugs at you. Cuts. Cuts.
I understand your fear, reluctance.
You had clung so tightly
Inside, attached so uncertainly to the womb
Against the tide of blood that threatened to sweep
    you away
Down the toilet where she sat, head bowed,
Watching the flood.
Bargaining for you (Yes: with that promise she keeps)
With the god she might as easily have cursed.
Except that it might be you who paid.
Cuts. Cuts. Your mother's flesh, muscle, fat, blood.
They tug and tug now
After you had held so tightly
In that micro-ocean, your gray eyes shut
In desperation, clinging to your only hope,
Yourself, imitating her position, her purpose,
Hugging and bowing into yourself,
Into your own stubborn strength,
Curving your feet so tightly against you
They would need casting,
The tide flowing, seeming to drain, leech you
Fair black child
You are free,
Out, I tell her, second daughter,

Dara. The Beautiful One, last
Child (before they close her)
Is free.

LIBERATION

It's one of those little mean
Coincidences our world turns on.
Only last night I read Sexton's
Celebration of her uterus,
And here I am this
Morning, sitting by
Without use in my wife's room
While the surgeons' hands work busily
Removing hers. And I celebrate
That sacred part of her
That has withstood, for mere human love,
The trials and crucifixions of her body.
Miscarriage and birth and
Miscarriage and birth and
Pain, and pain. I always said
"We" lost the baby, just as I said "We"
Have a daughter, but I could say nothing
About that pain. She lay there
In the middle of it, while I
Could only stumble
Around its
Edges,
Terrified of its
Vaguest touch. At the ends of our dark nights
Together, after her pain had shriveled
My little mortal soul to dust,
I could never decide which made the crueler joke:
God as male bungler
Or God as female masochist.
But the survivors were women,
She and the two Lovelies
Who clung to that sacred part
For mere human love, and were delivered.

And I celebrate that woman
Who stood bleeding two years
On her magnificent pillars
Like another wonder,
Bleeding her human blood,
Baptizing me as I crawled under her,
My belly lower than the ground.

And God, dam the blood of the lamb.
I celebrate the merely human bleeding womb
That brought salvation to us all.

GOD'S BUTTON

The god my child conceived of last night
Can press a button on a machine, she said,
And make you grow, even when you're sleeping.
The reality of an idea, as god is,
Is no less than that of a starfish or pinebox;
Its power may be greater than an earthquake, volcano,
Or no less than absolute, eternal.
So her improvisation must have caused
The drowsy inhabitants to jostle for room
To admit her Buttonpusher to the pantheon.

Then, "God is love," she said.
But the jury of my senses and I said No
If he is who must be absolute, eternal;
Love is not both—is more real than its idea—
But only human; we remembered the evidences
Of growing through catastrophes of gain and loss,
The "discontinuous phenomena" that shaped life's cusps
And surfaces when no truth, honor, pride, duty,
Or any idea, could resist any given moment,
Or even memory, of animal penetration and affection
(the way Helen walked pigeon-toed through the snow
made my choice between her life and another's;
remembered round pressures, the small warmths of faces
pressed between neck and shoulder;
voices dying away, fading,
human only).
God is love if eternally, continuously human,
Longer than the moment it took him to fake death,
Perverting it into faith, doctrine: Idea.

Love has made me grow, though not so straight
As the pines I saw through her window,
Waking her this morning. In the early sun
They were themselves spears of light growing up
As our lives run down.
Whose finger is on which button?
As mine runs down I make progress
In knowing one thing God is not.
Death is eternal, absolute, animal, human.
God is love as long as one of us lives.

THE DEATH OF ANOTHER FELLOW

1. It's April, the month I can't escape,
Thick with paradoxes, when
So many things have ended or begun.
I am pulling the lawn mower through the back door
When the sun blinks and freezes the space
Where my unwitting sinister eye sees the black shape
Vanishing between the two concrete blocks laid end to end
On the sloping earth beneath my window.

Now I unwillingly know the secret
Of his hiding place: he hadn't been far from home
When he'd left those shed skins
Along the rear wall of the house
Those years before. Not far at all.
And the warm driveway was his porch,
Where he'd surprised Helen
Once too often. It must be killed
Because of the girls, she told me.
How can she let them go out into the yard?

But until he became so careless
He never revealed where he lived.
And I swear: I thought I didn't know.

2. It's a simple, mindless chore, cutting grass.
You can easily lose yourself in meditation
Going back and forth across a yard
As I do this Sunday morning.
It's less easy if you're being constantly
Watched, back and forth,
As I am.

> *I know who you are, African forebear*
> *coming to give me corn and fertility;*

incarnation of our dead, unborn children;
Indian ancestor, great grandsire, spear
of the war gods, rain-bearer;
and you, the more "civilized" of my burdens,
tempting me with wisdom and guilt.

I have little enough of one, none of the other.
Because I wasn't meant to be alone
I married twice, but continued to burn.
Now there are old lost loves to remember,
To wonder what became of,
For whom I might have been cutting this grass.
And sons, who might have been doing it for me.

The farther away from him I get
The further he comes up, black and straight,
From between the stones, outlined
Against the house, watching me
In a curious, friendly way.
In spite of the enmity
It's hard to resist that functional beauty,
The symmetry of its purpose in living.

> *I see you, old buddy. At this distance*
> *are you following only the sound of the mower*
> *back and forth, or is it me?*

You play with fire. And your children burn.
For the love I found wholly incarnated in Cathy's arms,
Eve's breasts, Kay's hair, Suzy's lips,
Annie's thighs my sons burned without their father.
Alas, alas that ever love was sin!
But that *was* love, the better part of wisdom;
Nevertheless, why keep the grass cut
And the yard fenced in
And free of snakes if there are no children?

> *But you are inside the fence*
> *and that's as far as I can go*

before I must come back to you.
And still you rise from your hole
the farther away I go,
my fixed foot leaning after me
but vanishing if I approach you.
I need the distance more than you;
but there's this goddamned fence.

And here in the corner of the yard, the mowing
Is difficult where Helen had the garden plot
The year before the first baby was born.
The grass has overgrown it now, and surrounded
By the drainage ditch, and raised higher
Than the level of the yard, it resembles an island
Or burial mound.
But she made things grow there in profusion.
Lettuce, beans, tomatoes, squash, eggplant, corn.
And the fruit in the woods beyond the fence:
She never went over there, afraid of the snakes.
And she wants the yard free, her home safe.
I tell her

        he is harmless, and replaces
          small, lesser, more numerous, flabby evils

(and maintains a balance in my nature)
She says: it is better to marry than to burn,
But I was not meant to burn with you.
Nor will I let my children.

3. I leave the mower running out of his
sight, behind the redwood fence that extends
twelve feet from the wall of the
house into the yard.
I go into the basement for the
B.B. gun, a rake and spade, out the
front door around the side of the
house, behind him. At the corner of the

house I peer around, brace myself against the
house, and sight the gun on the opening
between the two blocks. His head emerges, waving
toward the sound of the still running
mower. I aim at the back of the
small head and try to stop wavering. I
miss the first shot and he
vanishes. I cock the gun, feeling cowardly, and
foolish, hoping no neighbors see me.
He emerges again and I steady
myself. Another
miss? So, I've got to face him.
I go through the gate, carrying my
rake and long-handled spade. I pull over one of the
concrete slabs with the rake, and then the
other, and in the hollow space underneath

> *from the mass of black coils*
> *the head comes up and the spade goes*
> chuk chuk chuk (*Stop!*) chuk chuk *through*
> > *the body*
> *into the cool clayey earth.*
> *The sun is blinking, freezing the images*
> *of his movements; his lidless, unblinking eyes*
> *mock and accuse me in cold intelligence,*
> *its sacrifice transforming it into Serpent.*
> *The head falls back among the coils and guts,*
> *the mouth opening and closing in gasps,*
> *as if to localize the pains.*
> A small movement. A nest? Young ones? A
> > family?
> No. Serpents are solitary, live alone.
> That is its tail.

I cover him with dirt,
Bury it there under my window and replace the stones.
It was so helpless after all,

So easy to kill.
And my own fears.

4. Now it's June. Walking up the front steps
With my oldest daughter, I hear rustling
In the dry leaves at the side of the porch.
I look over the wrought iron rail
And see a black snake, smaller than the one
I killed, moving along the front wall. Above it,
On a bush, a mockingbird is chirping at it
In agitation, feathers ruffled, wings outspread.
I take my child into the
House, tell her to stay there while I
Kill a snake. I get the spade from the basement
And go back out to the front yard.
It has gone. And so has the bird.
I go around the house and find nothing.
Back inside, my daughter asks if I killed it.
No. It was gone.
But Daddy, it was harmless anyway and wasn't
Going to hurt anybody.
I look at her, unbelieving. No, I said,
It wasn't going to hurt anybody.

> *Then what was it I killed, what is buried*
> *in the backyard under my window?*

Photo by Joan Barrax

GERALD BARRAX

Gerald Barrax was born in Attalla, Alabama, in 1933. At the age of ten, he moved to Pittsburgh, where he lived until 1969. He has studied at Duquesne University, the University of Pittsburgh, and the University of North Carolina (Chapel Hill). At present, he teaches English at North Carolina State University in Raleigh, where he lives with his wife, Joan, and their children. He is author of two other volumes of poetry, *Another Kind of Rain* (Pitt Poetry Series, 1970) and *An Audience of One* (University of Georgia Press, 1980). His poems have also appeared in numerous periodicals, including *Poetry*, *Black World*, *Southern Poetry Review*, *Journal of Black Poetry*, *The Georgia Review*, *Poetry Northwest*, *Essence*, and *Callaloo*.